NICOLSON

Best Walks
around
LOCH LOMOND

by Gilbert Summers

NICOLSON MAPS
N
3 Frazer St, Largs
Tel. 01475 689242

CONTENTS

Published by Nicolson
3 Frazer Street
Largs KA30 9HP
Tel: 01475 689242

First published 1998 by Collins
An imprint of HarperCollins*Publishers*
77-85 Fulham Palace Road
London W6 8JB

© HarperCollins*Publishers* 1998
Maps © Bartholomew Ltd 1998

The walks in this guide were first published in
Bartholomew's Walk Loch Lomond and the Trossachs.

ISBN 1 86097 064 8

MG10395

KEY MAP FOR THE WALKS

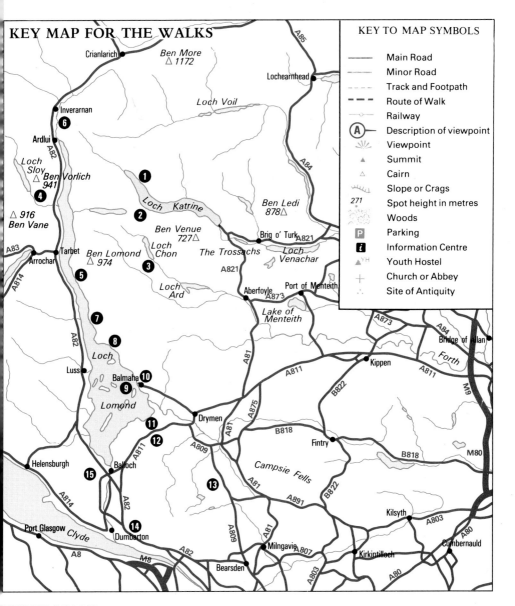

KEY TO MAP SYMBOLS

——	Main Road
~~	Minor Road
- - - -	Track and Footpath
▬ ▬ ▬	Route of Walk
—○—	Railway
(A)—	Description of viewpoint
☼	Viewpoint
▲	Summit
△	Cairn
ⱶⱶⱶ	Slope or Crags
271	Spot height in metres
∴	Woods
P	Parking
i	Information Centre
▲YH	Youth Hostel
+	Church or Abbey
∴	Site of Antiquity

Map labels

Crianlarich, Ben More △1172, Lochearnhead, Loch Voil, A85, A84, Inverarnan ⑥, Ardlui, Loch Sloy, Ben Vorlich △941 ④, Ben Vane △916, Loch Katrine ①, ②, Ben Ledi 878△, Ben Venue 727△, Brig o' Turk, A821, Loch Chon, Loch Venachar, The Trossachs, A82, Tarbet, Ben Lomond △974 ③, A821, Arrochar ⑤, A83, A814, Loch Ard ⑦, Aberfoyle A873, Port of Menteith, Lake of Menteith, A873, A84, Bridge of Allan, ⑧, Loch Lomond ⑨⑩, Luss, Balmaha, Kippen, Forth, A811, A811, M9, B822, Drymen ⑪⑫, B818, Fintry, B818, M80, Helensburgh, Balloch ⑮, A809, A875, Campsie Fells, M80, ⑬, Port Glasgow, Clyde, A814, Dumbarton ⑭, A82, Milngavie, A807, Kilsyth, A803, Cumbernauld, A80, A8, M8, Bearsden, Kirkintilloch, A803, A80

KEY TO SCALE

SCALE 1 : 63360

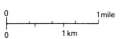

0 ————————— 1 mile

0 ————————— 1 km

SCALE 1 : 25000

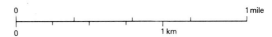

0 ————————— 1 mile

0 ————————— 1 km

3

INTRODUCTION

1 WALKS AROUND LOCH LOMOND

Loch Lomond is not only an outstanding area of natural beauty, but represents the flavour of the Highlands within a short journey of the densely populated lowlands. A hard grandeur, a troubled history and a (sometimes slightly eerie) sense of emptiness ensures that Loch Lomond is uniquely Scottish.

This book is for ordinary walkers who want a chance to stretch their legs in the fresh air, a place to park that does not make the driver uneasy, and a day out without too many worries about the uncomfortable questions of access, route-finding – or getting back in time for tea.

Loch Lomond, with its rugged and steeper terrain in the north and tendency to sprout 'private' notices in the south, has been covered partly by dipping into the West Highland Way, Scotland's first long-distance footpath. In this rugged area in particular, the walks have been chosen with care, bearing in mind the relatively inexperienced walker. Equally, they have been chosen to make the most of Loch Lomond's famed beauty – islands dot its water, Ben Lomond looms impressively on its eastern shore, and secret places still survive surprisingly close to the rush of traffic along the A82.

The selection is intended to be representative, rather than exhaustive – there are many more routes for walkers to discover for themselves. Though varying in length, the suggested routes have one feature in common – they should all be suitable for the reasonably fit walking party, wearing stout shoes or boots with well-cleated soles.

2 WHAT TO WEAR IN THE SCOTTISH COUNTRYSIDE – VARIED WEATHER PATTERNS

This section is not intended as a guide to what the sartorially-conscious walker will wear this season. (Most walkers are fairly idiosyncratic anyway and never stray far without their beloved woolly hat and sweater.) Winter walkers would be well advised to take an anorak or thick jacket, woolly hat, scarf, gloves and waterproof over-trousers. Inner clothing should comprise several thin layers, rather than one thick jumper, and warm trousers,

NOT jeans. As regards footwear, proper walking boots are preferable and, for some walks, essential, particularly where the individual texts mention wet or slippery paths. Even if boots are not worn, shoes *must* give good ankle support and have a well-cleated sole to provide grip. Country lanes and idyllic meadows are in short supply – replaced by terrain on a grander scale.

Summer walkers still need strong footwear, plus a light cagoule-type jacket, a spare sweater – and, summer, or not, the waterproof trousers or lightweight rain-suit might still be useful. Remember the vagaries of Scottish weather. Stunning colours, tumbling streams, lovely lochs mean, after all, water, in the form of rainfall that increases the further west you go, complicated by further increases the higher you climb. Mid-March to mid-June is, as the most daring of generalisations, often the driest period, though, personally speaking, September and October have much to recommend them. July and August are warmer, but statistically wetter. Remember, too, the rule of thumb that for each 1000ft (305m) climbed, there will be a drop of around 4 degrees F, with windspeeds likewise increasing. The best advice on clothing, therefore, is to be flexible. The average July temperature is around 58-59 degrees F. (14.44-15 degrees C).

A small word about a small problem – the infamous Highland Midge. Some visitors may have mused that there must have been a conspiracy of silence over this less-than-endearing feature of life in the Highlands. Certainly, few glossy tourism brochures give it any space, but it is fair to point out that in still conditions, on mild days near bodies of water in particular, the uniformly sadistic members of the Ceratopogonidae family may make their presence felt. Long-sleeved shirts are therefore preferable, and you are advised to carry a repellent, which usually needs frequent re-application. Different people react in differing degrees to their bites, but the attentions of any of the 29 different blood-sucking species can be a little annoying.

3 SAFETY FIRST IN THE SCOTTISH COUNTRYSIDE

It is always wise to have additional maps, covering a wider area than the intended walk and hence useful for identifying distant features. The 1:50 000 Ordnance Survey series is recommended, as is the *OS Tourist Map of Loch Lomond and the Trossachs*, while enthusiasts will appreciate the extra detail of the 1:25 000 series. A compass is also useful – essential if you deviate from these recommended routes. A plastic bag for maps is a good idea, or even better, a proper plastic map-holder with a cord strap as used by orienteering enthusiasts.

Learn the basics of map-reading. At least be able to orientate yourself by holding the compass on top of the map, folded to the relevant portion, and turning map, compass and yourself until the compass needle points to magnetic north. You should then be able to identify features in the landscape. If you do not have a compass then from a known point, line up the map with a more distant feature, such as a hill-top.

In assessing how long each walk should take, it is difficult to generalise – your decision-making must be based on the slowest member of the party. Pay most attention to the vertical rise given for some of the walks and allow extra time. Do not assume that the shortest distance will take the shortest time. Remember that all of the walks described are intended to be pleasurable outings – not too taxing and designed to allow for picnics, photography, botany, birdwatching and gazing at the views! If in doubt, choose a there-and-back again route and clearly note your starting time.

Many walkers, particularly if going high in winter, leave notes on the car dashboard with their routes and estimated return times. Although the walks in this book are generally modest in scale, do not feel embarrassed about adopting this practice. Likewise, let someone know at 'base' where you intend to go. Read each walk before you start off and pay close attention to warnings, particularly if boisterous children are in the party. Without dwelling overmuch on the gloomy aspects of the Scottish landscape, remember that smooth wet grass, twisted heather roots, old leaves, are all hazards even before you encounter the more obvious crags, rocky places, fast-flowing streams, slippery banks of lochs and other obstacles which contribute to the unique beauty of the Highlands.

A small first aid kit is invaluable for treating the occasional small cuts and bruises, and a whistle is useful for attracting attention should a more serious accident occur. If someone in the party does meet with an accident, ensure that when you reach a telephone, you give as precise details as possible of the location to the police and emergency services. But, to repeat, constant watchfulness is the best way to avoid this possibility, particularly as the walk nears its end and tired legs are less able to avoid pitfalls.

4 HOW THE WALKS ARE GRADED

Given that all the area can be described as rugged, to a greater or lesser extent, this leads on to the question of grading the walks. A walk that might be considered an easy jaunt for a party of fit hillwalkers, accustomed to relentless gradients, for the ordinary family on holiday would present more of a challenge. At the other extreme, even if a walk is graded Easy, remember that you are in Scotland, and that it is still advisable to be properly equipped.

The area, rather obviously, has lots of steep gradients – for those who seek them. However, to make for more relaxed walking, advantage has often been taken of the astonishing mileage of forestry roads in the area. Some of these have been waymarked by the Forestry Commission and this book takes the liberty of joining in and opting out of these markers to suit the purpose of the walk. Remember on the Forestry Commission's ground that their own activities may, from time to time, mean a particular route is temporarily out of bounds. Do not worry – there is a wide choice. Instead ponder upon the problems that might be encountered if there was not normally a fairly liberal attitude taken in Scotland to the crossing of land in private ownership.

5 THE LAW OF TRESPASS IN SCOTLAND

Read all the available literature on walking in Scotland and you can be forgiven for still feeling a little hazy on the question of the rights of the individual walker. At the one extreme there appear in print little guides which urge the determined walker to carry a thick polythene bag to help cross barbed-wire. One even suggests that in certain areas, the walker with a picnic would be well advised to choose a dense thicket in which to consume it! Other texts dismiss the whole business and blithely state that there is no law of trespass north of the border. This is incorrect. The law of trespass in Scotland concerns itself with possible damage while the trespasser is on private land. In practical terms, this means the onus is on the landowner to prove damage – but he or she is entitled to request you to leave his or her land by the shortest practical route.

Some of these walks take advantage of rights of way, which in Scotland are defined as routes between places of 'public resort' in use for a period of at least 20 years. However, the lack of certainty over the whole business has partly come about through the tolerant attitude shown by many landowners on the question of walkers on their land. Should you, while using this book, go wrong and stray from the recommended routes, you then bear full responsibility for ensuring that this fairly satisfactory relationship between most landowners and walkers in Scotland is maintained. Check locally for seasonal or temporary restrictions such as lambing or stalking. Your local Tourist Information Centre or Countryside Ranger Service will be able to assist.

6   THE COUNTRY CODE

Most walkers are responsible people, showing the appropriate degree of common sense with regard to countryside activities. Nevertheless, here is a reminder – the Country Code – as laid down by the Countryside Commission:

1   Enjoy the countryside and respect its life and work.

2   Guard against all risk of fire.

3   Fasten all gates.

4   Keep your dogs under close control.

5   Keep to public paths across farmland.

6   Use gates and stiles to cross fences, hedges and walls.

7   Leave livestock, crops and machinery alone.

8   Take your litter home.

9   Help to keep all water clean.

10   Protect wildlife, plants and trees.

11   Take special care on country roads.

12   Make no unnecessary noise.

Study the code closely and you will find it is a perfectly reasonable list of suggestions, imposing nothing whatsoever on the recreational countryside user. One or two aspects of it are particularly important for the area covered by this book. Keeping dogs under proper control is of great importance as many of the walks are in sheep country. Remember that under the *Civic Government (Scotland) Act* 1982 a farmer may shoot a dog which is about to attack livestock if there is no other means of restraining it at that moment. The law is on the farmer's side as he may then prosecute and claim damages from you as its erring owner for any injury or loss. (Roe deer, when very young, are also vulnerable to injury from roaming dogs.) You can see why it is simpler to keep your impetuous pet on a lead – and pay close attention to any warning notices in the lambing season.

Young birds, when just out of the nest, can draw attention to themselves by weak flight and unnatural tameness. Leave well alone – their parents will be along shortly with their next meal. And under the general heading of respect for wildlife and the countryside, do not disturb the nesting site of any wild bird. Similarly, picking wild flowers is frowned upon most severely – it is downright selfish anyway – and you might just meet a militant botanist.

Worth emphasising, too, is that surprisingly early in the year, forests can become a fire hazard and common sense must be exercised. Remember that your host for many of these walks is the Forestry Commission. Read their notices carefully.

7   GEOLOGY AND LANDSCAPE

The Highland Boundary Fault lies across the area covered in this book. It will be noticeable on many of the walks that the views give Highland and lowland contrasts. The fault line that separates the Highlands from the Scottish Midland Valley runs through Loch Lomond, Balmaha, the Menteith Hills, Loch Venachar and on, north-eastwards. Below it, the immediate lowlands are mainly sandstone on which very recent glacial action has dumped other rocks and gravels. Northwards, complicated bands of conglomerate, slates, and schistose grits are not easily comprehended by the amateur eye. As a simplification, it is enough to remember that the northern rock types are harder and more resistant to weathering than the sandstones immediately to the south. These northern Dalradian rocks (named after Dalradia, the first Scottish kingdom) are variable in appearance, some still showing their gritty origins on the floors of ancient seas, while others through heat and pressure have 'metamorphosed'. Probably the commonest are the schists, grey in appearance, sometimes streaked with parallel bands of other minerals.

The present-day landscape owes much to the differing degrees of hardness of these rocks, with the most resistant schistose grits forming the conspicuous bulk of Ben Lomond. After these ancient rock movements, much more recent Ice Ages (the last as recent as 10,000 years ago) stripped and plucked at the rough shapes, deepening and scouring valleys, dumping and damming to create major lochs such as Loch Lomond. Now, modern man has wrought other basic landscape changes. Electric power and water supply needs have resulted in the tampering with Lochs Sloy, Venachar, Katrine, Arklet, Drunkie and a few other waters in the vicinity.

8 HISTORY

Once, most of the area north of the Highland Boundary Fault was truly 'Highland' in the sense that its Celtic population lived by an economy adapted to a mountainous terrain. The clan system meant that families in any one community owed allegiance to the local chief. Some of the families would hold land as 'tacksmen' or relatives of the chief, others would pay rent in turn to these tacksmen. This system had evolved by about the mid-13th century. There was both a physical mountain barrier and a language separating these tribal units from the lowlands to the south.

Just over the barrier, the feudal barons were powerful. For example, Doune Castle, near Callander, was the centre of a large block of territory, held in the name of the Dukes of Albany. In those very distant times, the Earls of Lennox held sway over the south end of Loch Lomond from an earlier Balloch Castle. The Menteith Grahams were powerful in the area between. There is no space here to pursue the complexities of the area's history, but it must be said that the lowland landowners were not always successful in keeping the Highland clansmen from raiding southwards. Besides, for many of them, there were political careers to pursue elsewhere. News from their own tenants that yet another score of cattle had vanished into the mountains was extremely inconvenient. Things became so bad along the Highland/lowland border that, on occasion, the Scottish kings were even asked to intervene. From Edinburgh's Holyrood House in 1585 an edict was issued, summoning the local landowners to Stirling: 'The King and his council, being

informed that his good and peaceable subjects inhabiting the countries of Lennox, Menteith, Stirlingshire and Strathearn are heavily oppressed by reif, stouth and sorning and other crimes daily and nightly'. The three unfamiliar words mean plundering, theft and squatting – the last mentioned also involved using weapons to fend off any attempt to collect rent.

At one time sorning was a particular problem in Balquhidder Glen, though by the 17th century the glen was nominally controlled by the Murray family with headquarters in far away Blair Castle. Unquestionably, north of the Highland line, life was hard – little wonder that black cattle were lifted with regularity from the lowland fields. They provided a kind of welfare state on the hoof – a handy currency to see a family through a bad winter. One clansman who appreciated this from an early age was a certain Rob Roy Macgregor.

9 ROB ROY MACGREGOR

Rob Roy was born in Glen Gyle of the Clan Gregor, who at the time were being tolerated by a monarchy which had actually outlawed the entire clan earlier in the century, for the kind of reasons mentioned in section 8. His career cannot be separated from the time in which he lived. The reign of the Stuart monarchy was ending. Born in 1671, as a teenager Rob would hear of the succession of the House of Hanover, yet he remained a Jacobite (a supporter of the Stuart claimants) all his life, no doubt acquiring these sympathies from an early age through his own father who served in the army of the Stuart King Charles II.

He is remembered today, not just through the romantic portrait painted by Sir Walter Scott in his novel *Rob Roy*, but partly because in those lawless times, he, in effect, challenged the government, which in spite of all the resources of the 'British' army, was unable to bring him in. Sir Walter certainly saw him as the symbol of a Highland way of life, proud and independent, that was to vanish utterly with the advance of lowland 'civilisation' and the final dismantling of the clan system after Culloden in 1746.

The 'real' Rob Roy rose to notoriety through his dealings in the cattle trade, as a semi-legitimate drover, dealer and opportunist with one eye on the lowland herds. Superb swordsmanship, survival skills and the hill craft enabled him to defend property on the hoof, both his own and his 'clients'. This was noticed by the very powerful Duke of Montrose, who owned substantial grounds around Loch Lomond (and was a Hanoverian, too). A deal was struck. Rob was to use the Duke's money to buy and fatten cattle, with profits shared. However, the money disappeared while in the hands of one of Rob's own trusted drovers. Rather than give Rob time to repay the funds and with the most questionable of motives (Rob owned some lands on the east bank of Loch Lomond – now crossed by the West Highland Way), the Duke promptly declared him an outlaw and seized his house and lands. Thus, in 1712, a desperate phase of the Macgregor's life began.

He was, after all, 'hot property' – a man of skill and craft in an unstable political climate. He was within the sphere of operations of not only Montrose, but also another baron of high office – the Duke of Argyll, who was to command the government forces against the rebel Jacobites at Sheriffmuir three years later. Rob played a large part in this rebellion. Montrose wanted him to implicate Argyll in a Jacobite plot, with the return of Rob's lands if he bore false witness against Argyll, Montrose's political opponent.

He refused and instead redoubled his raiding on Montrose lands. He was captured on more than one occasion, but always managed to escape. Another major landowner, the Duke of Atholl, even managed to capture him through treachery, but Rob escaped again and made his way to Balquhidder. A network of sympathisers and intelligence gatherers plus supreme survival skills, meant that Rob, even after playing a part in the rebellion at Glenshiel in 1719, could gradually re-emerge to pursue the life of a cattle dealer, with a little semi-legitimate protectionism, in Balquhidder. There was eventually a reconciliation between all parties and Rob was to die peacefully in 1734. In his years of hardship as a fugitive, he paid the price for his refusal to become a part of lowland power squabbles, while remaining true to the Jacobite cause and evading all attempts to be brought to lowland justice.

10 THE LITERARY LANDSCAPE AND TOURISM

To Sir Walter Scott, talking on his journeys to old men who claimed as very young children

actually to have seen the revered Macgregor, here was the stuff of romance. Daniel Defoe thought so too, even earlier. (He would have heard such tales while living in Edinburgh, covertly helping with a spy ring which sent back information to Queen Anne, on the unrest in Scotland after the country lost its independence in 1707.) His *Adventures of a Highland Rogue* had assured Rob of fame in his own lifetime. But Scott could see, as he travelled in the area, that here was a land of vanished people, of a way of life that had no place as society was swept into the Industrial Revolution. His Rob Roy, symbolic of courage and honour, confronts a Baillie Nichol Jarvie representing lowland commerce and industry.

Scott was writing at a time of transition for the area. Though complex, the changes mainly came about through the impact of agricultural improvements in the lowlands, on a land already suffering from the aftermath of the post-Culloden political and social upheaval in the last half of the 18th century. Of the northern landowners, some with Jacobite loyalties had their lands forfeited after Culloden, while the rest were keen on introducing changes to the glens. The day of the black-face and cheviot sheep had arrived. Pasture that had grown oats and fed cattle for mainly local consumption was now nibbled down by ubiquitous sheep. Timber was cut to improve the sheep-walks. The creation of larger farms needing less labour meant that the glens soon emptied and emigration got under way, whether to cities or overseas – after all, a laird or chieftain now had no need to be able to call on numbers of armed kinsmen to defend his holdings.

Thus, when the Wordsworths visited the Trossachs on their Highland Tour in 1803, they already found an empty land. They clearly contributed to the cult of landscape. James Hogg journeyed here, too, and there were other travel narratives describing the wonders of this region on the edge of the mountains, even before the publication of Scott's *The Lady of the Lake* in 1810. It proved so successful that tourists flocked to see the sights and pick out the landscape features. Tourism was well under way.

Queen Victoria's love for the Highlands helped promote the fashion of visiting Scotland. In various parts of the country, the sporting possibilities of the moors were developed. Landowners could make money by leasing the land to sporting tenants, with any humbler tenants still remaining employed as ghillies. But as 20th-century wars and economic slumps also took their toll, these vast uplands were to prove simply not profitable.

11 FORESTRY ... AND MORE TOURISM

Forestry was the solution chosen to improve the fortunes of an upland area in decline. Now, along with a highly developed tourism industry, sweeping landscape changes have again taken place. There are historical precedents – the earlier Dukes of Montrose planted oak woods extensively in the Aberfoyle area. The bark was used in the tanning industry, itself obviously dependent on cattle. Now the state-owned Queen Elizabeth Forest Park, established in 1953, clothes the central area in the glaucous green of conifers. The acquisition of land of high landscape, but poor economic value, by the Forestry Commission started around the Trossachs and Loch Lomond areas in the 1920s.

The planting methods involve the ploughing of deep furrows and the placing of each young tree in the resultant upturned mound. You will see hill slopes where this activity has been quite recent and others where felling is under way. The dominant species are sitka and Norway spruce, with some Scots and lodge-pole pines on the drier areas. The walker will also find other firs and some oak and beech plantings, as well as semi-natural oak woods and birch scrub, the latter an indicator of the kind of landscape which would initially regenerate were it not for the sheep and deer.

It is no easy matter, coaxing economic returns on rocky slopes often deficient in phosphate and essential nutrients. Local populations of red and roe deer do not assist in this task, which is why deer-proof fences are often to be encountered, but at most places in the routes suggested in this book you will find deer-proof stiles, too. The walker, deep in the wind-rocked silence of tall pines, would be incorrect to assume that the trees around have been ignored since seedling stage. Far from it – cross drains go into the ploughed lands, then thinning takes place around 20 years later, and continues every five years until clear-felling is carried out after about 50 years of growth. Fertilizing or spraying may also be necessary – as well as the building of access roads for plantation maintenance and extraction. Yet in spite of all that, the forests are peaceful places.

Modern leisure needs overlap fairly well with forestry activities. The coach parties are quite satisfied with the sight of moorlands well-spiked by spruce at various stages of maturity. Car parks, picnic sites and forest trails are much in evidence around Loch Lomond. Under countryside legislation the Forestry Commission is, in fact, bound to 'have regard to the desirability of conserving the natural beauty and amenity of the countryside'. This is why there are few problems of access on its land, unless it conflicts with management activities, such as spraying or felling. Right across the area, there is a constant reminder of the statistic that 80 per cent of new planting in Britain is in Scotland.

Walk 1
GLEN GYLE AND LOCH KATRINE
10 miles (16km)   Easy

Take advantage of the fact that the road round most of Loch Katrine is open only to Strathclyde Water Board vehicles. Walkers (and cyclists) have it more or less to themselves, making it easy for extra cautious or ill-shod pedestrians to escape a little from the motor car. Most visitors discover this for themselves at the Trossachs car park at the east end; fewer, though, start their excursions from Stronachlachar pier in the west. While the former is the domain of Sir Walter Scott, Glen Gyle is the territory of the real Rob Roy Macgregor. If you are prepared to take a whole morning or an afternoon for the excursion, then walk round beyond Portnellan to a sad little graveyard, protected from the deepened waters. Here many of the clan sleep, their fields now flooded through industrial man's lowland needs. You pass the birthplace of Rob Roy on the way; it is now a private house. Another Macgregor graveyard is nearby. The skyline in the west now has pylons striding along it, where once the cattle were brought down for the lowland sales. As the black beasts passed by his front door, so to speak, it is little wonder that the young Rob decided that cattle would be his trade. Take plenty of film and stroll as far as time permits, keeping an eye on upper Glen Gyle for any changes in the weather. As Loch Katrine is a water supply, camping, bathing, fishing, boating are all definitely forbidden and picnicking is not encouraged - but for scenery like this, with the comfort of a properly surfaced road, it is a very small price to pay.

A As you start, from Stronachlachar pier, note Factor's Island, just offshore where Grahame of Killearn, the Duke of Montrose's factor, was held to ransom by Rob and his band. The island would have been larger before the water level was raised.

B Looking right, Ben An can be seen at the far end of the loch.

C View of Portnellan on the opposite bank, the site of the first house occupied by Rob Roy after his marriage. A little to the right can be seen what look like railings on the shore: this is the old Clan Gregor graveyard.

D First view of Glengyle House (private).

E This quiet part of Katrine is the haunt of surprising numbers of wildfowl. Any species showing a lot of white at this range might be either goosander - very white, but the male has a red bill, or goldeneye - with a fast wing beat, making the bird appear to flicker black and white, and a white patch at the base of its bill.

F Opposite Glengyle House, ahead lies upper Glen Gyle, with the old drove road following the line of the disfiguring pylons. (They come in from the Ben Cruachan Hydro-Electric Power scheme.) The hill blocking the end is Ben Ducteach; beyond lies Loch Lomond. A little further to the right is a pass in from upper Balquhidder, the Bealach nan Corp, suggesting that funeral parties made their way into this glen. Upper Glen Gyle, according to tradition, was also the site of a lost village. Everywhere, now, the hills have only sheep, though a few cattle are also grazed in the glen. Try to imagine the scene with much broader fields in front of the house and the east-west traffic of drovers and pedlars bringing life to this now empty valley.

G In wet weather, from the bridge, note the conspicuous waterfall, the Sput Dubh, coming off the crags high above Glengyle House.

H The causeway leads to the second graveyard. When the loch, raised by the waterworks, threatened to cover the original site of the stones, they were moved to their present site. This is the place where Wordsworth was inspired to write *Rob Roy's Grave*. Sadly, he was wrong, as Rob himself is buried at Balquhidder, but William and Dorothy were lucky to see these stones in their original positions, at least 10ft (3m) below the strange embankment on which they now appear. Donald Glas of Glengyle (Rob's uncle) is, however, thought to lie here, though time has quite defaced the inscriptions.

0   1 mile

0   1 km

5   *Just before the house itself, divert momentarily to the left, up an inconspicuous path in the trees and, with due respect, visit the first of the Clan Gregor burial grounds seen on the walk. Among the family buried here is a nephew of Rob Roy, Gregor 'Black Knee' Macgregor who was a chieftain. 'E'en do and spare not' reads one of the inscriptions, and visitors can also make out the symbol of the pine tree, torn out by the roots, part of the clan crest.*

4   *After passing The Dhu, the house on your left, the road makes its way round the head of the loch.*

6   *Continue past Glengyle House. (A door lintel has 'G. MacG 1704'.)*

7   *Continue past Portnellan (two old farmhouses) and look for a causeway, your turning point.*

8   *Retrace your steps all the way back to the Stronachlachar pier.*

3   *Take left fork to lochside.*

2   *Go up the road from the pier, turning right at the junction where the notice says 'No Unauthorised Vehicles'.*

1   *Park at the Stronachlachar car park, where the steamer calls. Reach this point by turning right at the western junction of the B829.*

11

Walk 2

LOCH KATRINE AND THE START OF THE AQUEDUCT

4.5 miles (7.5km)   Easy, though moderate when not on roadways

This walk follows the line, above ground, of a tunnel bored through the ridge that separates Loch Katrine from Loch Chon. It carries Glasgow's water supply on the start of its 26 mile (42km) journey from Loch Katrine and was started in 1855. Royal Cottage, which the walk skirts, is the draw-off point and was so named from Queen Victoria's visit in 1859 to open the works officially. The first part is along a metalled road where only the occasional Strathclyde Water Board vehicle will interrupt a delightful vista. Once over the rough ground of the ridge, the return walk is by a public road, only justifiable for the fine views of Arklet. Nevertheless, this is one of the most scenic routes to walk anywhere in the Trossachs. The solitude of the high ground is in contrast to the scene in the 1850s, when the area swarmed with gangs of navvies. Please note that the shafts mentioned along the length of tunnel are more strictly towers and it is quite impossible to see into them, let alone fall down them.

A The supply from Loch Arklet over the hill, right, drops down to the main reservoir, via a series of quite impressive, though entirely artificial, cascades dating from 1895. Looking the other way, Factor's Island lies just off the Stronachlachar pier, while in the east Ben An's distinctive hump marks the heart of the Trossachs.

B An open, ever-changing view of hill and loch. Cameras at the ready.

C Just before leaving the surfaced road, look back, west, across the loch where both Portnellan and Glengyle House can be seen. Each has associations with the Macgregors (see Walk 21).

D As you cross, look for the conspicuous shaft of the outgoing aqueduct. This looks like a circular, blank, stone-built tower. Beneath your feet are two tunnels, each of about 1½ miles (2.4km) length, taking water gently towards Frenich at the end of Loch Chon (Walk 3 traces the next section of aqueduct). Look up to the skyline, where a slightly surreal collection of other tower-like structures marks the course of this Victorian engineering feat.

E To reach this optional viewpoint, leave the path momentarily at an inconspicuous fork. The main path skirts the topmost knoll to the right, but on top, near another obelisk, there is a fine view towards the Balquhidder peaks, northwards, and an unexpected view of Ben Lomond to the south. Lock Arklet lies to the west.

F A splendid end-on view of Loch Arklet. This view must be one of the most constantly-changing in all the Highlands. Loch Lomond, lying out of sight beyond the end of Arklet, can often be in squalls, while the nearer loch is flooded with sunlight. Keep film for this one. Arklet itself was increased to three times its size in order to supplement supplies from Loch Katrine. While looking down this lonely glen, consider that in Rob Roy's day, there was a township of around twenty houses at Corriearklet, the settlement on the right hand or northern bank.

Walk 2

Loch Katrine and the start of the Aqueduct
continued

1 If driving, go right at the western junction of the B829 and park at the Stronachlachar car park, where the steamer calls. Go back up the drive, turn left, then second left to gain the road that runs along the south bank of Loch Katrine. The sign says 'Reservoir Area, No Unauthorised Vehicles'.

2 Continue along this picturesque surfaced road. It carries only Strathclyde Water Board traffic and follows the old drove road down Glen Gyle (at the far west end of Katrine) and over the Bealach nam Bo. Note, left, the hill passes on the far shore which the Macgregors would have used to travel to upper Balquhidder.

3 Just before the cattle grid, fence and wall, turn right, joining a track that goes up with the stream on your left.

4 Cross over little footbridge.

13 Take the third turning on the right to return to the pier.

5 Go over fence; the path is conspicuous enough.

6 After a short wettish section, go past a strange obelisk, devoid of any markings, presumably an aid to surveying the line of the tunnel. The path kinks uphill here.

12 Turn right at the road junction.

7 If dropping off the knoll, take care that you do not do so too literally, as the heather is steep and slippery.

8 Go over ladder-stile and into coniferous plantation.

9 At first shaft in the forest, take care to follow the path going left and into the woodland. This avoids the slippery slope beyond the shaft.

11 Turn right and be patient on this road section, the first part is less interesting and a little hemmed-in by conifers.

10 Follow this path back to the road, enjoying the stream which flows on the left.

Map labels

Stronachlachar · Jetty · Eilean Dharag (Factor's Island) · Aqueduct Outlet · Aqueduct Intake · Loch Arklet · B 829 · Cattle Grid · 271 Meall Meadhonach · Shaft · Royal Cottage · Pier · Boat House · Loch Katrine · Shaft · 278 Tom Ard · Shaft · Stuc Gille Chonnuill .392 · Faery Knoll · Lochan Mhàim nan Carn · Loch Chon · (A) (B) (C) (D) (E) (F)

Walk 3
AROUND LOCH CHON
6 miles (10km)   Easy

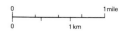

This is a walk which shows that the visitor need not stray too far from the public road to be rewarded with some solitude. Its gradients are negligible and the unexpected presence of an aqueduct keeps the interest up on the west bank where mature trees obscure some of the views. Loch Chon is said to be haunted by a dog-headed monster that swallows passers-by. This warning should ensure children are well-behaved on its banks. Other wildlife interest includes jays, buzzards and herons. This walk is one of a number of Forestry Commission routes within the Queen Elizabeth Forest Park, but it also approaches farmland at the loch's north end and **dogs should be very firmly on a lead**

---

13 Go through gap in wall, immediately after man made cave, giving aqueduct access - there is another obvious section of aqueduct nearby. Then cross stream close to another visible section.

12 On left, an identical shaft to that mentioned at F. Go straight on. This marks an approximate halfway point, about one and a half hours after leaving the carpark. The next section is through a pleasant, comparatively open ride.

11 Cross bridge and bear right.

10 Path plunges back into mature conifers, with a scattering of ancient oaks, and crosses two footbridges.

9 The next section has open views over loch and a gently rising and falling gradient.

8 Note path merging on right. White waymark is reassuring. Carry on to loch side.

7 On passing the last of the buildings on your right, look out on the same side for a narrow path, with a white waymark at the time of writing. This is your route. The path is hemmed in by tall trees and you may find it is rather slippery when it is wet.

---

1 Take the cul-de-sac road to Inversnaid from Aberfoyle. About 7 miles (11km) along it and after little Loch Dhu is the Loch Chon Car Park, signposted by the Forestry Commission. This is your starting point.

2 Walk back to the public road and turn right. When a sign to a boat launching place is seen, turn right down to the loch shore.

3 Turn left along a faint path, sometimes boggy underfoot. Cross a stream, following the bank of a twisty river connecting Lochs Chon and Dhu.

4 Beyond the tree, the path splits. Take the drier one, heading back towards the road.

5 At the road turn right.

6 Turn right at the Loch Dhu House road, passing notice board for waymarked trails, and go over bridge. Follow road to houses.

Map labels: Shaft, Shaft, B829, Quarry (disused), Foot Bridge, Frenich Farm, G, Shaft, F, H, Heron Island, E, Shafts, D, Aqueduct, P, A, Boathouse, Loch Chon, C, Loch Dhu, Loch Dhu House, B

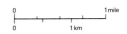

0   1 mile

0   1 km

15 This pleasant stretch of path continues through bracken till it reaches a track, which leads you to the main road. Note the view back to Ben Lomond from the track.

14 Third shaft and large stream come into view. Cross by the footbridge. Go through a small brown gate. DO NOT TURN RIGHT on to Frenich Farm property. Continue through 'kissing gate' - only a few paces further - and shortly reach an open ride.

21 Opposite the next island, the shore path becomes clearer, indicating your nearness to the car park and your starting point. Continue along it till it reaches the far end of the car park itself.

16 Rejoin public road which runs downhill and gives a view of Loch Chon. Turn right.

17 If time is short, it is quicker to keep to the road back to the car park. It is more interesting, however, to divert where possible, along the bank. The first of these opportunities comes with a bracken-covered wall. Follow it down to the shore to pick up faint path, passing picnic sites, then return to road, noting shortly after, an old milepost (Aberfoyle 8 miles, Stronachlachar 3¼). Make sure you are walking towards Aberfoyle!

18 Option to leave the road, following the bank closely, crossing stream and climbing fence almost immediately.

19 Only the faintest of paths hereabouts.

20 After walking round promontory, climb fence and find route along steep bank, reminding yourself it is only fifty yards up to the public road should the thick bracken exasperate.

A A splendid viewpoint by a magnificent oak where the river broadens into Loch Dhu. Note bridge at far end, which you will shortly cross.

B The pleasantly-scented wiry plant growing in the wet patches is bog myrtle. (Try it with pork chops.)

C At loch side, note Frenich Farm, your turning point at far end of loch.

D Wood sorrel, with clover-like leaves, grows below the larches after first footbridge.

E Overgrown spoil heaps on left indicate old tunnelling operations when aqueduct was built. Near the second footbridge a black iron-plated structure is a visible section of aqueduct. This carries water from Loch Katrine to Glasgow. On this shore, there are actually two separate aqueducts, of which the earlier, built in 1855, will become intermittently visible as the walk progresses. Beyond it, note common tormentil with its four small yellow petals and also the first of many short stone posts, indicating the position of the subterranean water channel.

F On left, note stone building, like a strange observatory with an iron lattice dome. This is an inspection shaft.

G Pause to admire open view northwards, with line of aqueduct disappearing towards Loch Katrine, over the hill range (Walk 2).

H Look out to Heron Island, a very logical place to expect to find these solitary fishers, though they are wary of disturbance.

15

Walk 4
THE LOCH SLOY DAM
7 miles (11.5km)   Easy; no dogs

Escape from the hubbub of the Loch Lomond traffic into the slightly unexpected tranquillity of a glen with looming mountains. Admittedly the scenery is marred by power lines in plenty - but the scale of the rocks and hills is large enough to dwarf even a 182 feet (56m) high dam, built in 1946, the first major project of the North of Scotland Hydro-Electric Board. The dam generates 130MW of electricity and meant the raising of Loch Sloy by 155 feet (47m), drowning for ever the old home-lands of the Clan MacFarlane in order to supply power to Central Scotland. In spite of these changes, the walk has much to recommend it and gives an opportunity to sample the wildness of the interior from the 'security' of a good road. You will not have to pay too much attention to navigation - there are more views than instructions - and the route is on a surfaced road nearly all the way, which you will only have to share with the occasional NSHEB service vehicle and more ambitious walkers heading for the tops of the looming 'Munros'. Like Walk 1, Glen Gyle, you could even take a push-chair! **Dogs are not advised - this is sheep country.**

A The Inveruglas Power Station with its less-than-beautiful four steel pipes (pre-dating the days of scenic consciousness!) receives water from Loch Sloy via a tunnel on the hill 2 miles (3.22km) long. The water drives four vertical turbo-alternators and then escapes into Loch Lomond.

B After noting the big hills that begin to dominate the landscape, you reach a strange humming complex behind wire on your left. This is a switching station. Power arrives here not only from Inveruglas but from two other hydro-electric schemes further west (in Glen Shira and upper Glen Fyne). It leaves via yet more pylons that stride south down Glen Loin, on your left, beyond the station.

C The nearest mountains are, left and continuously visible as you climb, A' Chrois (the end of a ridge that runs from Beinn Narnain); Ben Vane, conspicuous ahead, beyond the farm; the top of Ben Vorlich hiding behind the rocky shoulder immediately on your right; Beinn Ime, set further back in the glen between A' Chrois and Ben Vane.

D The dam is 1,170 feet (357m) long and 295,000 tonnes of crushed rock were used in the concrete. It was the first buttress-type dam in Scotland. Among those employed in its construction were prisoners of war awaiting repatriation, following the end of World War II. A temporary railway station was set up at Inveruglas to receive them.

E You then have a view of the dammed loch itself. Its shoreline scar is an inevitable result of the fluctuations in the water level. The catchment area was increased from 6.5 square miles (17sq km) to 31 square miles (80sq km) by means of tunnels and aqueducts. This is, admittedly, one of the wettest parts of Scotland - if it rains, remember that every inch of rain generates one million units of electricity!

F The insect-eating sundew is quite common in places among the mosses in the shallow ditch along the upper side of the road. Among the bird life, wheatears, with their distinctive white rumps, are also very conspicuous.

G On your way down there are fine views of the impressive cone of Ben Lomond. Equally impressive is the fact that during the last Ice Age, which ended a mere 10,000 years ago, a glacier carved out the trough of Loch Lomond right across the former watershed of the Inveruglas Water. This burn, which is the main one on your right as you make your way down the glen, would once have emptied itself eastwards, beyond Inversnaid, into Loch Katrine.

H Lower down, Inversnaid itself can be seen across the loch.

I Finally, as you reach the car park at the end of your walk, look out, right, to Inveruglas Isle, with the remains of a MacFarlane castle, sacked by Cromwell.

6 If you wish to see to the other side of it, follow the road round and uphill, past the buildings. Just before you reach the tunnel, detour left, leaving the path and going up and right, round the hillock through which the tunnel is driven. **DO NOT go into the tunnel.**

7 Retrace your steps to the road, which now, followed in the reverse direction, gives a completely different set of views. Consider how the Clan MacFarlane lived here, hemmed in by intimidating mountains, but with a comparatively rich pasture land, bright and green, on which to graze their cattle. Their war-cry was 'Loch Sloy', though it has changed much since their departure two hundred years ago.

1 Start from the large viewpoint car park on the shores of Loch Lomond, on the A82 just north of the Inveruglas Power Station, on the right. Turn left out of the car park and make your way back down the road, past the power station. Take care on the busy road, but there is a pavement or verge nearly all the way.

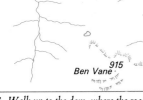

5 Walk up to the dam, where the road turns left across its base.

4 After the farm called Coiregrogain, (which can be seen off to the left of the road) go straight on at the road junction to see the dam. It comes into view ahead as the road swings north with the bulk of Ben Vane looming on your left. You also lose sight of Beinn Ime, behind Vane's shoulder.

3 Go straight on, past the switching station, at the junction of three roads, i.e., take the middle road.

2 After Inveruglas Farm, on the left, turn right into a driveway, conspicuous by its notices warning about no parking, no unauthorised vehicles, no dogs on the hill. Go through the gate and under the railway bridge. This is on the main road to the dam. Continue up.

17

Walk 5
LOCH LOMOND WOODS
8.5 miles (13.5km)   Some easy, some moderate, a few difficult places

The rugged nature of the Highland landscape often prevents the link-up of a satisfying circular route, but north of Rowardennan there is the unusual opportunity of taking in two versions of the West Highland Way. The high road is a forestry access road and, like all the others frequently encountered on the walks in this book, is easy both in gradient and underfoot. However, the low road is another matter. It twists through the oakwoods, presenting widely differing grades of walking from deluxe smoothed gravel to rocky shelves which the management powers have seen fit to supply with chained handrails for the timid. The whole route as described leaves the public road at Rowardennan and, after three-quarters of an hour's walking, gives you the choice of which half of the loop you wish to do first. The easier high track offers good viewpoints across to the high hills around Arrochar, while the low path offers adventure and, perhaps, even an encounter with (shy) wild goats! The walk as described goes out by the easy road, back by the more strenuous route. The turning point is an optional half-hour extension to the Rowchoish bothy, a shelter intended for the long-distance brigade, midway between Rowardenn and and Inversnaid. This is quite a big day out; make sure you are fully provisioned and equipped.

A If you can ignore the traffic noise from the opposite bank, even before you reac Ptarmigan Lodge, the woodlands typify the sentiment of the famous song about the 'bonnie banks'. The prolific bird population seems to think so too and a spring walk here is very rewarding. Garden warblers seem particularly common and can be recognised through being utterly devoid of any markings whatsoever - just a general dingy grey-brown. Their song, however, more than makes up for their less-than-exotic appearance.

B Notice the rhododendrons in this section, so beloved of west-coast landowners for privacy purposes. An alien species, rhododendrons are common all over the west of Scotland. As you walk along, consider how resistant they are to any efforts to get rid of them. Their glossy leaves resist chemical spraying, their wood is not easily burnt, and if cut down, they spring from the base. They destroy all ground cover and provide little or no food for birds. Even their nectar is poisonous and domestic animals will not graze them.

C The Cobbler to the north-west shows its spectacular silhouette near the ruined sheilings. Notice how the track has temporarily climbed up out of the oak woodlands that flank the loch into the spruce plantations higher up the hillside - some aspects of the view will be lost as the conifers grow.

D A momentary diversion to the left offers a fine view down the loch.

E ...and even better mountain views north-westward if you peer between the birches. Ben Narnain is flat-topped, next to The Cobbler, with Ben Vorlich further north.

F Go down to the shore for a low-level viewpoint at Rowchoish bothy. Good views northwards. Inversnaid, with public road access, is on the east bank. In hazy conditions, you can just make out the coaches that have made it down the hill. Across the water is Tarbet with the West Highland railway-line coming over from Loch Long on its way to Oban or Fort William and Mallaig. The Cobbler is still prominent on the skyline. The scenery is splendid - but the summer season traffic noise echoes across the waters on a still day.

G All around you and stretching away north are the lands of Craigroystan, once owned by Rob Roy Macgregor, at the height of his 'legitimate' career. As you make your way through the oaks it is hard to imagine that, according to 18th-century documents, one hundred and fifty families had their homes in the little townships scattered between Rowardennan and the head of the loch. Land once tilled has now returned to a kind of wilderness.

H Do not be surprised if you come across wild goats hereabouts; their ancestors have been here for generations.

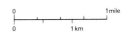

0   1 mile

0   1 km

7   *After retracing your steps from Rowchoish, stay on the bank this time, following the West Highland Way signs.*

6   *If intending to walk the Rowchoish detour, go right where the track peters out on the shore. You are on the West Highland Way. (Otherwise, go left, following on from point 7.)*

5   *At the fork go left to Rowchoish and the lochside.*

4   *Shortly after the first of the Arrochar Hills appears ahead on the far bank of Loch Lomond, on the left of the track you will see the start of the low-level section. Make your choice here. The route suggested continues on the higher track.*

8   *The path climbs above the rocky drop known as Rob Roy's prison, where, it is said, he held his opponents confined, or even that he lowered them over the slabs into the water. Many stories attached themselves to him; sufficient to say that it is an odd spot, particularly on a still day, when it seems hard to work out exactly how far away the water is - take care not to lean out too far!*

9   *Grey wagtails, tree creepers, sandpipers, bluebells, creeping jenny - all small distractions on a path that varies from well-gravelled to slippery and rocky. Please try to keep to a single track; lazy walkers searching for slightly easier ground on either side of a minor obstacle are the ones responsible for spreading of the main path.*

3   *Go right and uphill at the fork and through a gate.*

2   *Make sure you continue right at the Youth Hostel fork, then left at the next fork, noting a West Highland Way marker.*

10   *In many places, falling in to the loch would take more than a reasonable amount of silliness, but at this point it is enough of a possibility to justify the chained hand rail.*

11   *The path clearly climbs left and back up to the forestry road. At the road, turn right and retrace your steps.*

1   *The walk starts from the well-used Rowardennan car park, the terminus of the public road. Go northwards along the track from the car park.*

Map labels:

Tarbet — Pier
Rowchoish
F
Creag à 492 Bhocain
E
G
H
Rob Roy's Prison
D
C
Ben Lomond 974
731 Ptarmigan
A82
B
Ptarmigan Lodge
A
A82
Rowardennan Lodge
Rowardennan
Pier
P
Jetties
Caravan site
Rowardennan Hotel
Caravan site
Inverbeg
Y.H.

Loch Lomond

Walk 6

INVERARNAN - LOCH LOMOND VIEWS
4.5 miles (7.5km)   Moderate (easy in places)

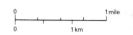

A walk that takes advantage of an attractive part of the West Highland Way to gain a wonderful end-on view of Loch Lomond. It lies near ancient ways through the hills, used by cattle-drovers before the coming of the railways ended their trade.

The area once supplied timber for iron smelting; the old Caledonian pine forest reached one of its most southerly limits in nearby glen Falloch. Later, after the tourists arrived, the river that runs parallel to the walk described here was canalised

between the end of Loch Lomond and the Inverarnan Hotel. Steamers connected with stagecoaches at the hotel, which is also your starting point.

2   Taking care on the main road, turn right from the car park and walk a few hundred yards along the road as far as the first bridge over the River Falloch. Turn right, cross the bridge and go right again over a stile. At time of writing this had West Highland Way indicators.

1   The Inverarnan Hotel has welcomed generations of walkers and climbers and is on the right as you go north, on the A82 beyond where Loch Lomond ends and Glen Falloch begins. Park in the car park.

3   Continue along the pleasant river bank till the path meets the Ben Glas Burn (which has a fine waterfall

much higher up the hillside). Then turn upstream and over a tall ladder-stile.

4   Turn right over stile and cross the newish footbridge, built by the Royal Engineers. Follow the path south till it almost rejoins the River Falloch.

5   Path forks; go upwards and left.

6   Go through the ruined walls of the hamlet of Blarstainge, evidence that this deserted east side of Glen Falloch once supported a much higher population.

7   As you approch the Dubh Lochan, the 'little black loch' on your right, look out for a diversion, newly made at time of writing and intended to prevent path damage. The sign takes you upwards to the left, off the original path which stayed on the level.

8   You may wish to make this a longer expedition by continuing down, eventually to reach the oak woods by the loch itself. There are also views across to Ardlui. Otherwise, retrace your steps back to Inverarnan.

A   If walking this route (and most other walks in this book) in moist weather in springtime, there may be a pleasing scent in the greenest of woodland, which does not come from any blossom. This is the scent given off by new birch leaves. You may notice it now as the path climbs into the birches.

B   High above and out of sight, left,

is the old drovers' route down to Glen Gyle from Glen Falloch. Rob Roy would have known it well.

C   In the wetter patches, butter-wort, an insectivorous plant (like sundew) may be found. It looks like a little fleshy green starfish.

D   From the hamlet, looking northwards up Glen Falloch, Ben

Lui and Ben Oss are conspicuous, as is the nearer Ben Vorlich, south-wards and on the other side of Loch Lomond.

E   From the top, a magnificent view of Loch Lomond, lying in its narrow glacial trough, open out. Island I Vow is conspicuous.

Walk 7

ROWARDENNAN WATERFALL

2 miles (3.5km)   Moderate

```
0                                              1 mile
|___|___|___|___|___|___|___|___|___|
0                              1 km
```

Walks from Rowardennan, by the nature of the landscape, are of two kinds; either quite long, as in Ben Lomond, or the Loch Lomond Woods walk (Walk 5) or quite short, as in this hour-and-a-half's worth of scrambling about in the woodlands. The walk is of interest for the difference between the two sorts of path that it uses. The first is - or was at time of writing - a little overgrown, but well-constructed, climbing steadily by the banks of the Ardess Burn through delightful wooded scenery with pleasing waterfalls. The second path, used on the way downhill, is the walkers' 'motorway' to and from Ben Lomond and, with its erosion problems, makes an interesting contrast. (The route to the top of 'The Ben' is first recorded in Ordnance Survey maps of the 1860s and '70s. Like other hills further east in the Trossachs, it had the proper credentials to attract the tourist, even in Victorian times. It was fairly accessible, a conspicuous objective and the highest point in the vicinity.) Take care on the way down if it is wet.

---

3 *Though there has been a stream below you, right, the path crosses another.*

4 *The oaks are left behind as you enter a thick plantation with scrubby birch growing closely round the path.*

5 *Continue to push steadily upwards, enjoying the scent of the bog myrtle crushed underfoot and intermittent glimpses of the slopes of Ben Lomond - as well as the tumbling Ardess Burn.*

Rowardennan Lodge
L o c h
Rowardennan
Ardess Burn
Waterfall

2 *Before you reach the first fork (the left-hand track of which goes to the Youth Hostel) take a faint path going uphill on your right, into the oaks. It may be waymarked.*

B   C
A
D

6 *Path leaves the noise of the waters behind and swings momentarily right into thick conifers in an unexpectedly southerly direction before emerging on the main Ben Lomond path. Be prepared to stoop low under some of the encroaching conifers.*

L o m o n d
P

Rowardennan Hotel

1 *The large car park at Rowardennan is the starting point. Go northwards along the shore road that leads towards the Youth Hostel.*

8 *The path swings you right and away from the firebreak; follow the path down to the car park.*

7 *Go left and downwards. Glen Douglas is conspicuous straight ahead on the other side of the loch.*

A Shortly after, there is a good view from a firebreak back over to Loch Lomond as well as to the Sput Ban, the white waterfall, conspicuous in wet weather on the flanks of Ben Lomond above.

B There is a short digression possible here to another waterfall. Look for a point where the path broadens and climbs gently away right. The waterfall is reached by a faint path off left. Return to main path after viewing it.

C Another fine view over your shoulder down to the loch and the Youth Hostel, now surprisingly far below you.

D Road improvements, continuing high ownership of private vehicles, forestry interests channelling walkers in certain areas, and guidebooks, too, have all contributed to the obvious heavy usage to be noted on the main Lomond path; yet a recent report by The Countryside Commission for Scotland considers this path to have been in worse condition forty years ago. Note how the walkers are now, at least, kept in one line, rather than allowed to follow a wide number of 'braided' pathways.

21

Walk 8

SALLOCHY WOOD AND THE BANKS OF LOCH LOMOND   2.5 miles (4km)   Easy

Sample the famous banks of Loch Lomond without committing too much energy and time to the excursion. Walkers seeking more exercise in more rugged scenery should look at Walk 5, beyond Rowardennan. First-time visitors along this section of the Balmaha-Rowardennan road will find the celebrated shoreline an interesting combination of private property and public recreation areas, which has caused some headaches for the planners of the West Highland Way. This little walk takes advantage of part of a forestry trail, then joins the West Highland way for the return. It is an excursion on which even the habitual stern warning about footwear might just be suspended! Take care, though, on slippery tree-roots in the plantation and also near the viewpoint on the banks of Loch Lomond. Enjoy the birdsong of the oakwoods - from May onwards, dedicated birdwatchers will be sorting out the songs of wood warbler, garden warbler, redstart and tree-pipit, while the rest of the party will be enjoying the views across to Inchlonaig - the island of the yew trees, which were said to have been planted by Robert the Bruce to supply the Scottish bowmen.

2 *Park and follow the nature trail signs away from the loch and across the road, noting the change of woodland into managed plantation - which at time of writing has helpful little nameplates on some of the trees.*

3 *Just after the labelled western red cedar, the path takes you into the trees. Watch for slippery roots.*

4 *You pass the ruined hamlet of Wester Sallochy, swamped by gloomy conifers. Follow the signs left, twisting past the old walls, then go right and up.*

5 *You emerge on to a forestry road. If you continue on the waymarked trail, it takes you left to higher viewpoints beyond an old quarry, seen on the left. Instead, GO RIGHT on the forestry track.*

1 *On the continuation of the B837 4 miles (6.4km) north of Balmaha, look for the road signs to the Sallochy Wood car park, your starting point.*

6 *Cross the main road and on the shore side, look for a track heading down to the water's edge.*

10 *Enjoy this well-maintained final section back to the car park.*

9 *Follow the leftmost of two paths back to the shore.*

8 *To avoid a rocky outcrop, the path kinks right and up.*

7 *The path very soon joins the West Highland Way. Go right.*

A Strathcashel Point is in view as you stroll gently down the track.

B Very pleasing, open woodland with honeysuckle underfoot.

C A splendid viewpoint south to Inchlonaig and the other islands beyond. Luss is the village on the far bank. In summer, note the dense oak canopy immediately below. On the shore, peeping sandpipers are common in spring before too many visitors arrive.

Map labels: Sallochy Wood, Quarry, Rowardennan, Forest, Wester Sallochy, Allt a' Mhoine, Allt a' Mhorain, Dhuirgan Burn, Loch Lomond, Sallochy

Walk 9

INCHCAILLOCH
2.5 miles (4km)   Mostly easy

This walk is a little different from the others: it is on an island. Inchcailloch can be reached by using the services of MacFarlane and Son, The Boatyard, Balmaha, Loch Lomond, G63 0JG, Tel: (01360) 870214. They run an on-demand ferry service to Inchcailloch, in addition to cruises on the loch, which also call at Inchcailloch by arrangement. Phone them with the numbers in your party and arrange a suitable time. You can trot round the island in just over an hour (it is bigger than it first appears) but it is suggested you spend, at the very least, two hours, to soak up the atmosphere, enjoy the superb summit views, picnic, take pictures etc.

Inchcailloch is owned by the Nature Conservancy Council and the greatest respect must be paid to its woodlands: keep to the paths, keep your dog under the strictest control, and read the notice on landing. There is an excellent nature trail booklet available.

6 *Veer right and uphill to a diversion left to the 13th-century church, evidence of the vanished community. From here it is only a few minutes walk down left, then left again, back to the shore and the landing stage on the right.*

1 *Park in the main Balmaha car park, on the right going north. Go back and cross the main road.*

Opposite is a road down to the loch. Go down the road, turning right for the pier and the departure point.

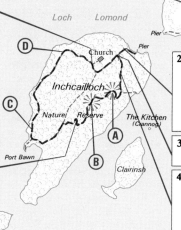

2 *Disembark at North Bay. If the loch is high, there is a path going right, a few yards up the slope, otherwise walk along the shore to pick up the main path running into the wooded island.*

3 *Turn left and cross a stream by a footbridge.*

4 *The oaks are replaced by alder trees where it is wet. Note how these alders have several trunks, suggesting they have been coppiced some time ago. Keep on the main path.*

5 *The path, mainly constructed of railway sleepers, leads down to a junction. (There is the remains of a corn-drying kiln on the right of the path just before the junction, at the foot of the slope; it looks like an old drain.) Go left to the slightly unexpected camp-site at Port Bawn (written permission needed to camp) then back along the shore.*

A On your way to this viewpoint, there is a face of the lumpy conglomerate sandstone (familiar if you have already walked on Conic Hill). Higher up you look south to the island of Clairinsh (with its 'crannog', a 2000-year-old, man-made island at its left-most tip) and beyond to the Endrick marshes. Behind these are the Fintry Hills then (right), the Campsies and the Kilpatricks.

B But an even better view is to follow, looking north to the Highlands from the 250ft (75m) high summit: a huge panorama of island and mountain.

C Like Conic Hill, Inchcailloch has a band of serpentine running parallel to and north of the fault line. This metamorphic rock, seen in an outcrop just left of the path, looks dingy and is smoother than the conglomerate.

D The site of Inchcailloch Farm. Although the entire island, thickly wooded, looks natural, the oaks are mature trees that have grown up from the managed woodland which was a source of oak bark, used in the tanning industry. This stage in the history of Inchcailloch was from about 1770 till the end of the 19th century. Before that, the island was farmed; the Nature Conservancy Council's nature trail booklet gives further information.

Walk 10
CONIC HILL
3 miles (5km) + 1130ft (345m)   Mostly difficult; no dogs allowed

Conic Hill rises behind Balmaha on Loch Lomond. Though higher, it seems to match the shape of the islands that rise in a line from it out into the loch. Geologically, this is unsurprising as Conic Hill and the islands lie on the Highland Boundary Fault. Stand on its summit and you can truly look on two different landscapes and cultures. This walk takes advantage of part of the West Highland Way, but escapes it, as it becomes boggy, to ascend a little way for a switchback walk back along the rather confusing line of tops. The conglomerate rock of which the hill is constructed is a great geological pudding-mix. A red sandstone matrix holds together stained and water-rounded pebbles of various sizes, commonly of quartz and associated with the fault line. It can be a little treacherous to walk over; take care while descending the slope on the last of the hill's convex humps. There are continuous views all the way from the top of the pass (called a 'bealach' in Gaelic) and the walk is naturally most rewarding in clear weather. When driving towards the hill on the B837, pause at a convenient layby a mile or so short of Balmaha to study the profile of the hill, seen on the right. Your path goes along the skyline.

A Self-heal is the small purplish flower with a dense head. St John's Wort is taller, about 12 inches (30cms), with several yellow starry flowerheads. They grow along the track in high summer.

B Listen for thin high mewing - buzzards calling! They are common on the moorland around the hill.

C The distinct texture of the conglomerate rock is already apparent on the hill shoulder ahead. Note Stockie Muir in the distance, right, with the rocky line of the approach to The Whangie (Walk 13). The nearer dome of Duncryne Hill (Walk 12) at the south end of Loch Lomond is conspicuous behind the marshes of the Endrick mouth.

D As the path flattens out, there are the first views over long moorland slopes towards Ben Lomond, left, with the Arrochar Hills beyond, on the other side of the loch. Almost immediately, look for a short pathway joining from the heights above right. This is where you will rejoin later.

E From this top there are two tops visible looking back south-west, as well as a wide prospect of Loch Lomond itself. Look beyond the islands in line; in clear conditions the hills of Arran are visible beyond the Clyde, a distance of more than 40 miles (65km). In the opposite direction, try to pick out the Wallace Monument, on its crag beside Stirling. Southwards, the tower-blocks of Glasgow can also be seen, between the Kilpatricks and the Campsies. There are Highlands to the right and lowlands to the left - a very obvious contrast in landscapes.

F A last view of the islands without tops intruding. Inchcailloch is nearest, with Clairinsh just to the left, then, going out, Torrinch, Creinch and Inchmurrin. Notice how Ben Bowie on the far bank also lines up, marking the fault line. But it was the much more recent Ice Age, only ending 10,000 years ago, that carved out the loch in front of you, scouring a deep (600 feet; 183m) trench in the schists to the north, then broadening out where it met the lowland sandstones to form a shallower lowland loch of only around 75 feet (23m) depth. The dumped material from the glacier has kept the sea out, but Loch Lomond is only 27ft (8m) above sea level. Just as the Inveruglas Water (Loch Sloy, Walk 34) once drained eastwards, so the rivers in Glen Douglas and Glen Luss (up the loch on the far bank) once drained eastwards into the valley now occupied by the Endrick, until the Loch Lomond glacier cut through their courses. Now the Endrick flows west.

7 Keep to the waymarked path while it continues to ascend gently, with the bulk of the hill blocking all views on the right. Note that there are other paths or sheep tracks disappearing up to the right.

8 AT THE HIGHEST POINT of the West Highland Way proper (where underfoot in wet weather it resembles peat broth) leave it for a short path that goes up and right on to a little pass between two areas of higher ground. Here there is another path. Go left.

9 You should now have reached the most easterly high top of Conic Hill. There is a small cairn.

6 Make your way round to the top of the 'bealach' or pass.

5 The path, which started level, bends upwards and left by way of some de-luxe steps. Cross the stream at the top of the slope.

4 Go through kissing gate, noting lambing notices and warnings to keep to the path.

3 Take the second on the left and where track ends take the continuing path through mature conifers. Note the old Scots pine mixed with the tall larches.

2 Follow West Highland Way arrows (and a blue forest walk sign).

10 There is a faint and intermittent summit path. Follow it westwards along the line of the tops. (They can be a little confusing - there usually seems to be one more than you expect!) Note as you set off that the next top but one seems about the same height as your departure point. There are, however, four of roughly the same height.

11 Take great care on this lower top, where the path is lost among the knobbly rock. You will see the West Highland Way just below you.

12 You join the main path by going off right, at the top of the bealach. At time of writing there is a prominent pole. This is the path noted at point C on your way up.

1 There is a large car park in Balmaha, on the right going north. The walk starts from behind it. Go on to a forestry track and turn right.

13 Retrace your steps to the car park.

Conic Hill 361

Bealach Ard

Balmaha Plantation

Loch Lomond

Inchcailloch

Jetties

Pier

Balmaha

B837

Auchingyle

The Kitchen (Crannog)

Walk 11

GARTOCHARN AND
THE BANKS OF LOCH LOMOND 3.5 miles (5.5km) Easy

One of the easiest walks in this book, Gartocharn, bypassed by most of the tourist hurly-burly, sits contentedly in a patchwork of little fields, An important feature of the walk is its little foray into Shore Wood, part of the Loch Lomond National Nature

Reserve. This reserve, in the care of the Nature Conservancy Council, consists of five islands - Creinch, Torrinch, Clairinsh, Aber Isle and Inchcailloch, all clearly seen from the shore - and a substantial part of the marshes around the mouth of the

Endrick Water. Please note, only a part of Shore Wood is open without permission and it is important to keep strictly to the shore path. **Do not take dogs into the reserve and keep them on a lead while crossing fields.**

10 *A suggested turning point is in the vicinity of a second stile. Retrace your steps all the way back to the post-box at the junction at point 6.*

9 *Enter reserve at left-hand gate (carefully closing it behind you). Keep to the path, crossing a stile.*

8 *At next junction take left fork and follow the track down to the bank of the loch. After admiring the view from the water's edge, return to the track, going left to gate of reserve.*

11 *At post box turn right and follow road on.*

7 *At first junction, go straight on. At time of writing this was signed for the nature reserve.*

12 *Turn left at main road, left again by the toilets and so return to your starting point.*

6 *Look for a small post-box only about 100 yards (91m) further on. Turn right down track signed as a private road to a number of lochside houses.*

1 *Gartocharn is on the A811 south of Loch Lomond. Park sensibly in the village; there is some parking near the church, reached by turning left (if coming from Balloch) at the public toilets and following the road round to the right past the Police Station. The community centre is beyond the church to the east. Park, then go past the community centre and turn immediately left down the track beside the centre. Go through a kissing gate.*

5 *The path goes down a short track, over second little bridge and through a gate on to a surfaced road. Turn right, then left at end of road.*

4 *Do not cross fence; continue to follow field boundary till you reach a gate and a little railway-sleeper bridge on your left.*

2 *Follow faint track down through field, keeping boundary hedge on your right.*

3 *Track goes right and through kissing gate. Stream appears left.*

A Immediately a view of Loch Lomond opens up. Note the craft moored at Balmaha on the right-hand side of the loch and Ben Lomond dominating beyond.

Aber Isle is the nearest small islet. Moving west, Torrinch and Creinch line up along the Highland Boundary Fault, with a confusion of islands beyond.

further east as well as the oak dominant woodland have now been lost in the lowlands, because of the needs of agriculture.

B Given clear weather, this south bank offers fine views up the loch. Inchcailloch lies next to Balmaha with Clairinsh in front of it, though

C This reserve is important as it represents what was once a much more extensive habitat in Scotland. Most marshes like the one lying

D After crossing stile, visitors in May will enjoy a sheet of bluebells flowering before the dense oak canopy begins to cut down the sunlight.

Walk 12
DUNCRYNE HILL
2 miles (3.5km) maximum Easy

Duncryne Hill itself is probably the shortest walk in the book, which is quite unfair, as it also has one of the best views! Combine this walk with one to the shores of Loch Lomond (Walk 11). On arrival at the edge of the wood that surrounds the western part of this extinct volcano, there is a neatly-lettered notice which reads: 'Duncryne is private. Well-behaved visitors are welcome to use the track and hill-top. Please do not wander into the woods (reserved for teddy-bears etc.) Help us by clearing litter, left by less tidy visitors. We hope you enjoy sharing our point of view.' No finer summary of the Country Code can be found. Duncryne Hill is first cousin to Dumbarton Rock, Dumgoyne and a number of other volcanic vents, that is, the inner core of a volcano, a whole series of which were responsible for the ancient Clyde Plateau lavas from which the Kilpatricks and Campsies (seen prominently from the top) are formed. Duncryne itself pokes through the Old Red Sandstone; fertile fields surround it, in spite of its position on the Highland edge. Its little dome is unmistakable, from whichever compass point you approach Gartocharn.

1 *Gartocharn is on the A811 south of Loch Lomond. Park sensibly in the village; there is some parking near the church, reached by turning left (if coming from Balloch) at the public toilets and following the road round to the right. This is the same parking place as used for Gartocharn and Loch Lomond (Walk 11). Go back to the main road, turn left, cross over and take first right, before the speed limit signs, just past the Gartocharn Hotel. Go up this quiet country road for about half a mile and look for a layby, left, at the very end of the woodland also on the left. Alternatively, if time is short, drive here and make this your starting point.*

4 *Retrace your steps to the village, noting that the reverse of the same notice at the layby on the return says 'Ladies and Gentlemen, if you have been, we thank you'!*

3 *A path leads right from the kissing gate, then left and straight to the top.*

2 *Teddy-bears or not, a stile gives access to the wood edge with its splendid notice, and another leads to an open field. Go straight across to the kissing gate.*

A The view is quite unexpected and out of all proportion to the 470ft (142m) height. Nothing intrudes in the uninterrupted vista over the Highland Boundary Fault and into the high hills beyond. Between the Ochils in the east and the Clyde westward, the view encompasses the Perthshire Hills such as Ben More and Stobinian, round to the prominent Ben Lomond, Ben Vorlich (next left) and on to The Cobbler, and the Cowal Hills further west. But it is the loch and its islands that are most striking. Sea shells have been found in the terminal moraines, the materials dumped by glaciers, at the south end of the loch. This suggests that before the last Ice Age, the sea intruded up the Vale of Leven, seen conspicuously left. The last advance of the glaciers caused a wide dam of deposited material to form after they finally melted and withdrew. Only 27ft (8m) above sea level, Loch Lomond thus nearly became a sea loch like nearby Loch Long, a long fjord pointing far into the hills.

Walk 13
THE WHANGIE
3 miles (5km)   Moderate; no dogs

The Whangie has been well-known to generations of Glasgow rock-climbers. This strange geological phenomenon offers a wide variety of short but interesting pitches. For the walker it has scenic attractions, too, and is ideal for a short afternoon or evening's walk, enjoying views of Loch Lomond from these northern slopes of the Kilpatrick Hills. As for the geological reason for this peculiar, slightly eerie, even claustrophobic cleft, one explanation is an earthquake, while the information notice at the start of the walk also suggests glacial plucking. (This is stage one in the formation of a corrie, which is itself the hollow or valley scooped out of the side of a mountain by the passage of a glacier. Extremes of temperature at the head of the valley freeze rock slabs into the ice, which then 'plucks' them away and down the line of the glacier.) There is a third explanation for the geological peculiarities of The Whangie. The Devil was in such a state of anticipation as he flew to a witches' meeting somewhere in the north, that he lashed his tail and carved off the rock slice through which the path now goes. It might even explain the odd atmosphere that surrounds the place, though given a fine evening you might not notice it. Concentrate instead on the larks, the curlews and the Queen's View from the car park, where you will have to leave your dog. It is also the place, because of its popularity, to see fashion footwear at its worst. Do not attempt this walk in high heels.

A Note the hump of Dumgoyne, eastwards on the edge of the Fintry Hills.

B The view from the path, hemmed in between the fence below and the crags on your left, improves as you make your way towards The Whangie, as yet unseen. This is skylark country. Note the other little hump of Duncryne Hill, beyond the Stockie Muir, the moorland straight ahead, but in front of Loch Lomond to the north-west.

C Considering the nearness of the city of Glasgow, from the triangulation point there is a wide prospect over wild moorland, with Dumbarton Muir and the Kilpatricks to west and south.

D You are now inside The Whangie with vertical rock walls rising on both sides. There is a gap that gives a fine view north-west to Loch Lomond.

E The small birds that show grey buff, a black eye-stripe and conspicuous white rump are wheatears, common in summer along this section. The bird's name is derived from Anglo-Saxon and literally means 'white-arse'.

F For full details of the range of hill visible, check the excellent viewpoint indicator in the car-park.

0   1 mile

0   1 km

8 As you re-emerge, take the lowest path that you can find, going right and back along the face of the hill, retracing your footsteps to the ladder stile and down to the car park.

1 The walk starts from a well-marked parking place and large car park about 7 miles (11.2km) north of Bearsden, Glasgow, on the A809 to Drymen. Alternatively, if travelling from Drymen, look for the site about 6 miles (9.6km) to the south, on the right.

7 You enter by an unpromising-looking path which seems to disappear into the rock face.

Fort

Quarries

E

F

P

The Whangie

D

B

A   Queen's View

A809

353
Auchineden
Hill

C

6 You should find falling ground on both sides. Look for crags starting again on your right. This is the 'back door' of The Whangie.

Auchineden

2 The path is unmistakable: though the gap in the wall, past the information notice and uphill to the conifers ahead on the skyline.

5 A number of trails wonder away from the triangulation point. If you go straight ahead, towards two reservoirs, then you will overshoot The Whangie and have to descend a steep west-facing section after only a few minutes, then divert sharp right along a faint path. It is better to leave the top by going half-right on a path that leads off in a westerly direction.

4 Check that you are on a path which rises above a second line of rocks which start below you, right. As you near the top, a path comes in to join from your left. This is the one mentioned in point 3 that runs along the hill-top. Continue to triangulation point on Auchineden Hill.

3 With most of the uphill section over, you reach a ladder stile; go over it. From here a number of paths diverge, including one that runs along the top of the line of crags that goes off to your left. In unkind weather, however, it is easier to take the path that runs along the foot of these rocks. Do not lose height.

29

Walk 14
OVERTOUN AND THE KILPATRICKS
3-9 miles (5-14 km), depending upon route   Easy (low loop) to Moderate

The policies of Overtoun Estate offer countryside pleasures only minutes from Dumbarton and the A82. Further uphill in Forestry Commission ground, the walk around the Lang Craigs opens up views extending from the Renfrew Hills and the Clyde Estuary to the panorama of Loch Lomond. **Note:**

no dogs allowed at Overtoun, and stout footwear should be worn if continuing to the Lang Craigs, where younger children should be closely supervised by a responsible adult. There are several options for this walk, giving a choice between a short stroll or a longer ramble. Starting from the Police

Headquarters off the A82, the easy loop around the Overtoun policies can be enjoyed on its own, or linked into a longer walk continuing to the Lang Craigs viewpoint. Alternatively, the Craigs can be approached more directly from Milton, just outside Dumbarton or the A82.

3 *There is a choice of either driveway or footpath beside Overtoun Burn. If on the driveway, you eventually leave it by turning right through a picnic area, when close to a large farmhouse on the left.*

4 *Path climbs steeply up steps, left to Spardie Linn, a waterfall.*

5 *Cross footbridge on right, noting the sandstone in the stream bed above the falls, and follow the path upstream to regain the driveway. Cross the burn by the impressive bridge leading to Overtoun House. N.B. cars can be taken as far as Overtoun House by turning north off the A82 at Milton, opposite the garage. Now continue along the driveway as it bears right around the house to reach the estate entrance at a sharp bend in the minor road up from Milton.*

2 *Walking to the A82, go right, past the Police Headquarters, then immediately right again, through the old gates of Overtoun Estate. Continue up the pedestrian-only path, crossing over a housing estate road and entering the policies proper.*

6 *From here, you can easily return to your starting point by turning right, see point 14 overleaf. Otherwise, carry on up the road ahead, passing Loch Bowie on your right. Beyond the loch, at a sharp Y-junction, turn left and go uphill. (N.B. this section of the walk can also be approached by parking at Milton and walking up Milton Brae, opposite the garage on the A82, following part of the road to the car park at Overtoun House mentioned above.)*

1 *Park on the north side of the A82 dual carriageway west of Dumbuck Quarry, between the Pinetrees Hotel and the Police Headquarters in an estate of wood-faced houses. Take care on the busy main road.*

0   1 mile

0   1 km

12 *Path and fence lead up beyond the forest and on to the rim of the Lang Craigs where there are red grouse and spectacular views. Keeping the fence between you and the cliff face, continue by the path along the tops, crossing an intervening forestry fence by a stile. WARNING: This is no place for very small children.*

11 *Noting a small waterfall in the gorge on your right, follow the path for about ¼ mile (½ km) to a wire fence with a stile. DO NOT CONTINUE ACROSS THE STILE, but turn left, following the smaller path, which becomes clearer further on uphill with the fence on your right.*

10 *After a mile or so of gentle climbing, the track ends at Black Linn Reservoir, on your right, with the cone of Doughnot Hill appearing beyond the trees. Take the smaller path in front of you, with the fence on your right for 20 -30 yards (18 -27 m), before the path veers left through a break in the trees. (Doughnot Hill should now be on your right.) N.B. from this point on, the path can be slippery and boggy in damp weather.*

3 *The Craigs turn south. Path swings left, below a rocky bluff. Cross a second fence by a stile. Path cuts left and uphill, then right and picks up fenceline again (60 yards/55m). Continue down by the fence and then a wall bearing right to regain first gate crossed at start of upper loop. Retrace steps to Y-junction. Go left down road to Milton, or right to entrance to Overtoun House.*

9 *Continue following the main track through the coniferous plantations, passing reservoirs first on your right and then to the left.*

4 *If returning to the A82 near the Police Headquarters, turn downhill from the Overtoun gateway and then follow the track till it narrows and becomes a path. Keep heading downhill to the estate adjoining the main road. Turn right, past the Pinetrees Hotel, and it is a couple of minutes to your starting point.*

7 *Follow the road uphill to Greenland Farm. Then bear left by the metalled track which continues uphill to reach quarry workings. Take a rest here and look back; you should begin to see Renfrewshire, the Clyde Estuary and even Loch Lomond.*

8 *With quarry on right, and fence left, continue uphill past a brick hut. Track crosses an iron gate, then fords the burn by stepping stones, before striking uphill across a second gate towards forestry plantations. The Craigs are now visible ahead to your left.*

By the burnside, note the ruins of power-house, remains of an early example of hydro-electric power for domestic use.

The rock at Spardie Linn is known as Spout of Ballagan sandstone from a prominent outcrop in the

Campsies). This forms a lip over which the water tumbles, wearing away the soft shales and cementstones beneath.

C The views from the Lang Craigs are remarkable for a relatively small hill. Dumbarton Rock and the Vale

of Leven communities are clear below, with Glasgow spreading out to the south-east and Greenock and Gourock across the Clyde Estuary. Best of all is the open view right up Loch Lomond, as it runs north into the Highlands.

Map labels: Round Wood, Overtoun Burn, Quarry, Sheepfold, Lang Craigs, Waterfall, Black Linn Reservoir, Reservoir, Aqueduct, Overtoun House, Reservoir, Spardie Linn, Police Headquarters, Loch Bowie, Quarry, Reservoir, Greenland Farm, Quarry, Dumbarton, Dumbarton Castle, Milton, A814, A82

Walk 15
STONEYMOLLAN - LOCH LOMOND VIEWS
4 miles (6.5km)   Easy, but on moderate gradient; no dogs

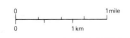

This is a walk missed by most visitors whizzing up the A82 Loch Lomond route. It shows how suddenly the countryside changes, from the industrial and housing estates of the Vale of Leven to the wilder moorlands of the Highland edge. Although it is a there-and-back-again route, keeping to the right of way, the views are splendid, and it would make a fine summer evening walk, should you be staying in the vicinity. This is sheep country, so please **no dogs**.

---

1 *Finding the starting point is the trickiest part of the walk. It lies on the old main road. You must first get to the roundabout situated between the bridge over the River Leven and the A811's junction with the A82 (which is also a roundabout, at the end of the dual carriageway, if coming from Dumbarton.) If coming along the dual carriageway, go right at the junction roundabout and left at the next. If coming from the east along the A811, go right at the second of the Balloch roundabouts. At the time of writing, the old main road going north towards Loch Lomond is signed for the caravan park. Park by the roadside beyond the caravan park seen on your left. (N.B. From the Dumbarton direction, just before the junction roundabout, the footbridge you will be crossing at the start of the walk is seen ahead.)*

---

8 *Go through another gate at the end of the plantation. Walk a little way down the track, then on to the slope on your left for the last viewpoint.*

9 *Retrace your steps to your parking place.*

7 *Go through the gate and enter the conifer plantation.*

6 *Stay near the boundary fence, keeping it on your right.*

5 *At Upper Stoneymollan, you leave the tarred road behind, going straight ahead through a gate. The woodland is also left behind as the landscape changes to a pleasant, open, brackeny hillside with a burn flowing down on the left.*

2 *Look for the road on the left called 'Lower Stoneymollan Road' between two cottages. It is just after the caravan park.*

3 *Go straight along this road till you reach the pedestrian footbridge over the main Loch Lomond road.*

4 *Cross the bridge and bear right uphill (not sharp right, a private driveway).*

A The views of Loch Lomond improve the higher you walk up this tarred road.

B Sheep country. With the sheep's close nibbling of grasses, bracken thrives where they graze, its seed carried on their fleeces.

C Forestry. Another cash-crop takes priority. Pause to look back to the Highland Boundary Fault, running its knobbly way along the line of the islands and into Conic Hill, Walk 10. (All this is below, i.e., right of Ben Lomond, the most conspicuous mountain in view.) The change from Old Red Sandstone (southwards) to harder Dalradian Schists (northwards) can be traced by the hummocks that run to the horizon, north-eastwards. Note, further left, the distant hills of upper Balquhidder, still to the right of Ben Lomond.

D Looking ahead and westwards, the profile of the Arran Hills (the so-called 'Sleeping Warrior') lies on the horizon to the south-west beyond the River Clyde and Port Glasgow.